13 Easy Tomato Recipes

Nature's Lycopene Rich Superfood
For Heart Health and
Cancer Protection

(What's for Dinner Series)

Joyce Zborower, M.A.

Copyright © 2013 Joyce Zborower
All Rights Reserved

ISMN = 1492296892
ISBN-13 = 978-1492295891

Joyce Zborower, M.A.

DEDICATION

I first learned how to cook by sitting at the kitchen table while my mother was preparing our food and watching her and later, by trying to do it myself while she watched and guided me. Many times, it was a pinch of this and a dash of that as we didn't always exactly follow the recipes. And that's what I hope you do with these recipes. Make them your own.

This book is dedicated to my mother.

Table of Contents

History of the Tomato	9
Plant Toxicity	11
Baked Stuffed Tomatoes	14
Brown Stew	16
Chili Con Carne	18
Cream of Tomato Soup	19
Fresh Tomato Sauce for Pasta	21
Kitchen Sink Meatloaf – with variations	22
Lasagna	24
Macaroni Salad with Tomatoes, Bell Pepper, and Red Onion	26
Mom's Spaghetti Sauce with Meatballs	28
Tomato Avocado Salad	30
Tomato Bisque	32
Tomato Pie	33
Tomato Sandwich	35
EXCERPT from How To Eat Healthy . . . foods to eat - foods to avoid by Joyce Zborower	36
CONTEMPORARY MALNUTRITION	36
Kindle Recipes	41
Disclaimer	41
One Last Thing	42
References	43

Joyce Zborower, M.A.

13 Easy Tomato Recipes

Nature's Lycopene Rich Superfood
for Heart Health and
Cancer Protection

The tomato (*Lycopersicon lycopersicum*) has been dubbed a super nutrient food because of its anticancer properties. Its lycopene protects against deadly prostate cancer. Cherry tomatoes are especially rich in flavonoids which are easily absorbed by the body and are very good at helping to protect the heart.

The tomato has become a very important garden variety plant. It is widely cultivated as a food plant in temperate regions. There are literally hundreds of different varieties of tomatoes. Anyone wanting to grow their own should be able to find a suitable variety for their region.

Usually, tomatoes prefer to be planted in the same spot year after year using the decaying remains of former plantings as their fertilizer. However, if the plants are plagued by disease it's best to discard the dead plants and choose a new spot for the next planting. Carrots make a good companion plant for tomatoes.

Four plants can produce enough fruit to feed a family of four for the entire growing season.

History of the Tomato

The tomato originated in either Mexico or Peru, experts are uncertain which, and spread throughout the world possibly by Christopher Columbus or Cortez bringing it back to their home countries during the 14th or 15th century.

The people back then were well aware of the lethal nature of the nightshade plants and for a long time the fruit was also thought to be lethal. They were cultivated as ornamentals or curiosities and were not accepted as food plants until the late 1600s. Today, tomatoes are a major crop of world commerce and an essential supplier of nutrients in the human diet.

Tomatoes can be red or yellow or orange depending on their variety. They all provide useful sources of vitamins C and E.

Vitamin C helps in the body's ability to absorb iron. (See Iron, above). It is also one of the anti-oxidant vitamins; it protects water soluble substances from being oxidized and turned into a free radical (cancer causing agent) by being oxidized itself.

Vitamin C is the most easily destroyed of all the vitamins. Examples: cut fruit exposed to oxygen can lose vitamin C. Heat (above 70 degrees F) will destroy it, and since vitamin C is a water-soluble vitamin, it leaks out into the cooking water. The use of cast iron pans in cooking will destroy vitamin C as will keeping it frozen for longer than 2 months.

Fruits and vegetables are best eaten fresh. To preserve the vitamin C in fresh fruits and vegetables store them in the refrigerator; cover cut surfaces with plastic film or aluminum foil; steaming or stir-frying are preferred methods for cooking vegetables for retention of vitamin C; cook vegetables only until tender (not mushy – do not overcook); add vegetables to cooked dishes near the end of the cooking time; serve the cooking water as soup or stew.

Symptoms of vitamin C deficiency include:
1. bleeding gums
2. easily bruised because the small blood vessels are more fragile and more easily broken, and bruises take a long time to heal
3. anemia – The advice of a doctor should be sought in all instances where anemia is suspected.
4. infections are common (i.e., a weakened immune system)
5. severe deficiency can lead to a disease called scurvy

Vitamin E is a fat soluble vitamin which means the body's ability to absorb vitamin E depends on an adequate fat intake from various foods. Its antioxidant properties help protect the body from free-radicals which are molecules that steal electrons from other molecules. Antioxidants donate an electron to the free radical making it stable, i.e. making it harmless.

"Vitamin E may help protect against cardiovascular diseases by defending against LDL oxidation and artery clogging plaque formation."

Tomatoes were recently declared a superfood when their heart health levels of flavonoids were discovered. While all tomatoes have heart health flavonoids, cherry tomatoes are especially rich in them.

The primary phytochemical in tomatoes is lycopene. High intake of lycopene from tomatoes is linked to a reduced risk of stomach, colon, prostate and rectal cancers. Lycopene is most easily absorbed from tomatoes that have been heat processed in some way.

Plant Toxicity

The tomato, originally introduced from South America, is a hairy herb of the nightshade family. Every part of the tomato plant (leaves, vines, sprouts) is poisonous except for the fruit. The poison contained in this plant is the "violently toxic alkaloid solanine". It is found primarily in the vines, but may also be present in the green fruit. "Poisonings have resulted from drinking tea made from the leaves."

Symptoms of solanine poisoning include:
    Headache

Stomach pain
Vomiting
Diarrhea
Very low body temperature
Circulatory and respiratory depression

Tomato plants have been known to cause dermatitis in susceptible individuals. Edible members of the nightshade family include: tomatoes, potatoes, bell peppers and eggplants.

Poisonings can be accidental or deliberate. To prevent accidental poisonings, when growing these plants be vigilant in keeping young children or pets from sampling its leaves.

Deliberate poisonings with these plants have been known since before the time of Christ. During the Middle Ages, 14th and 15th centuries, it was possible to hire a professional poisoner if one didn't want to do the deed himself. Famous assassins (e.g. Agrippina and Lucrezia Borgia) used poisons from the nightshade family for political or monetary gain.

13 Easy Tomato Recipes

Baked Stuffed Tomatoes

The anti-prostate cancer agent, lycopene, is prominent in this dish because the tomatoes are being heated. You also get the vitamins C and E. Brown rice is a whole grain and is more nutritious than white polished rice. It also takes longer to cook. Butter adds the fat necessary for the vitamin E to be absorbed by the body. It, along with the cheese, adds vitamin B12 for maintaining healthy nerves.

Here's what you'll need to have on hand:
    4 firm ripe tomatoes
    1 cup chopped mushrooms
    1 T chopped yellow onion
    1 T chopped celery
    5 T unsalted butter
    1 cup cooked brown rice
    Salt and pepper
    1 T chopped flat leaf Italian parsley
    1 cup grated Cheddar cheese

Cut tomatoes in half and scoop out centers. Discard seeds. Chop pulp. Melt 3 T butter in skillet; add mushrooms, onion, celery, pulp and sauté for about 10 minutes until soft but not brown. Add cooked rice, salt and pepper, parsley. Mix well. Fill tomato halves and top with about 1 cup Cheddar cheese. Dot with remaining 2 T butter and bake in moderate oven (375°F) for 20 to 30 minutes or until lightly browned. Serves 4.

How to Cook Brown Rice
    1 cup spring water
    1/2 cup brown rice, washed
    1 T unsalted butter

Put all ingredients in 1 quart pot. Cover. Bring to boil. Reduce heat and simmer until all liquid has been absorbed and rice is tender – about 45 minutes to 1 hour.

Brown Stew

The tomatoes give this stew a very special flavor though you can do it without the tomatoes.

Garlic has antibacterial and anticancer properties and promotes heart health. Carrots stimulate the immune system and are helpful in reducing the risk of lung cancer. Potatoes provide a useful source of vitamin C and iron and produce healthy energy. (Green or sprouted potatoes can be toxic.) Onion has anti-inflammatory and anticancer properties and is linked to a reduced risk of heart disease.

2 lbs beef stew meat (beef chuck) cut into bite-size chunks
2 T butter
4 cups boiling water
1 8 oz can tomatoes
1 T lemon juice – fresh, frozen, or canned
1 tsp Worcestershire sauce
1 lg clove fresh garlic, minced
1 medium onion, chopped
1 – 2 bay leaves
small pinch salt (optional)
1 – 2 tsp honey
½ tsp black pepper
1 ½ tsp paprika
dash ground cloves or allspice (I use cloves)
6 – 10 carrots – peeled and cut into chunks
3 – 6 potatoes – cut into bite-size pieces
1 lb (18 – 24) small white onions, peeled

Thoroughly brown meat on all sides in hot fat. (1 layer deep in lg stew pot)

Add veggies and continue browning until they get covered with the brown juices.
Add spices and continue browning a little longer.
The above gives everything a really good flavor.
Add boiling water, tomatoes, lemon juice and Worcestershire sauce….. and anything you haven't already added.
Cover and simmer gently for about 45 minutes to 1 hour.
Remove bay leaves.
Makes 6 – 8 servings.

Chili Con Carne (chili with meat)

This is an extremely easy-to-prepare meal. Basically, just put everything in your pot and let it simmer, covered, for 2 hours stirring occasionally.

You get the antioxidant lycopene with the tomatoes, vitamin B12 with the meat and butter, and protein with the meat and beans.

1 ½ lb ground beef
2 - 3 T butter
1 lg onion - chopped
1 - 2 cloves fresh garlic
1 green pepper -- chopped
pinch red pepper flakes (with seeds)
1 - 3 drops Tabasco
dash paprika
dash cayenne pepper
3 whole cloves
1 - 2 bay leaves
1 - 3 T chili powder
3 - 5 lg. cans chopped tomatoes (the more tomatoes you use, the more you need to increase some of the other ingredients)
(Add a little water to the cans to rinse out all the tomato juice. Add this to your pot.)
1 lg can or 2 regular-size cans dark red kidney beans - including liquid.

Brown meat, onions, garlic, green pepper in hot butter. Spoon off excess fat. Add remaining ingredients. Simmer 2 hours adding extra water if needed.
Makes 6+ servings.

Cream of Tomato Soup

This soup can be made with either canned or fresh tomatoes.

As with everything 'tomato', you get vitamins C and E, fiber, anticancer effects, heart protection, and lycopene because the tomatoes are being heated. The lycopene helps protect against prostate cancer.

Here's what you'll need:
    3 T unsalted butter
    1 small onion, diced
    1 stalk celery, diced
    1 sprig fresh Italian flat leaf parsley
    Pinch of thyme
    5 – 6 fresh red ripe tomatoes, blanched, skinned, cubed
or 1 lg can tomatoes
    Salt and pepper, to taste
    1 1/2 cups chicken stock
    3 T whole wheat flour
    1 1/2 cups whole milk
    1 cup cream
    1 fresh tomato, blanched, skinned, seeded, shredded
    Parsley, basil or chives for garnish

Melt 3 T butter in saucepan. Add onion, celery, parsley and thyme. Cook slowly about 5 minutes. Add tomatoes, salt and pepper, and chicken stock. Simmer covered for 15 minutes. Blend together 3T flour with 1 1/2 cups cold milk. Add to pot and stir until mixture comes to a boil. Simmer 5 minutes then strain. Press juice through strainer. Discard pulp. Add cream and reheat.

Taste for seasoning. Add shredded tomato. Garnish. Serve. Serves 6.

How to Blanch Tomatoes
Bring a pot of water to the boil.
Dip tomato into boiling water for about 1 minute.
Remove tomato and peel with sharp knife.
The skin should just about fall off. If not, dip the tomato again.

Fresh Tomato Sauce for Pasta

This is a recipe for those who may prefer something a little less structured. Play with it.

5 – 6 plum tomatoes – Peal, squish w/hands
Add fresh garlic and olive oil and fresh herbs

Grill chicken breasts with garlic and olive oil
Remove chicken from pan
Sauté in same pan – mushrooms, onions, green pepper – (optional: broccoli, spinach, etc.)
Chop chicken
Add chicken to pan w/ veggies. Reheat.

While this is cooking, boil pasta. Strain. Do not rinse. Put in bowl.

Add sauté mixture into raw tomatoes.

Add to hot pasta. Mix.

Grate fresh Parmesan and Osiago into tomato mixture. Add fresh, soft Mozzarella. . . . Enjoy!

Kitchen Sink Meatloaf – with variations

Kitchen sink meatloaf is a basic recipe that can be used as the starting point for a number of different dishes. For example, it can be meatloaf – or, it can be made into meatballs for spaghetti and meatballs – or, if mixed with cooked rice and simmered in a tomato/rice sauce, it becomes porcupine meatballs. Each variation will be discussed further following the basic meatloaf recipe

The meat provides needed vitamin B12, an essential vitamin that the body does not produce on its own. When using rice, use brown rice. It's more nutritious than polished white rice and also has a lower glycemic index, which means it won't spike your blood sugar.

Here's what you'll need for the basic meat mixture:
   2 – 3 slices of bread, can be fresh or dried
   Some milk
   1 – 2 eggs
   1/4 yellow onion, diced
   2 garlic cloves, minced
   Flat leaf Italian parsley, fresh or dried
   Sweet basil or Tai basil, fresh or dried
   Oregano, fresh or dried
   1/4cup Heinz™ catsup
   Freshly ground black pepper
   1 pound lean ground beef

Break the bread into pieces in a large mixing bowl. Dribble enough milk over it to moisten. Add remaining ingredients. Using your hand, mix thoroughly until well blended.

For meatloaf:
Place meat mixture in 9" x 5" x 3" Pyrex™ baking dish. Shape into loaf form. Squirt extra catsup over top of loaf. Bake at 350°F for about 1 hour. Pour off excess fat. Slice and serve. I usually bake some potatoes (either red new potatoes or sweet potatoes) in the oven at the same time.

For meatballs:
Form meat mixture into medium size balls. Brown on all sides in hot oil in a frying pan. Place in pot with simmering spaghetti sauce. Cook 15 to 20 minutes.

For porcupine meatballs:
Add 1 – 2 cups cooked brown rice to meat mixture. Mix thoroughly. Form into balls. Brown on all sides in hot oil in a frying pan. Add 16 oz can tomatoes, spices, more cooked brown rice, and potatoes (peeled, sliced lengthwise). Simmer 45 minutes to 1 hour.

Lasagna

Lasagna is one of those recipes that looks daunting but really isn't as long as you follow the instructions. The three separate parts get put together to make one very delicious meal. . . . And it makes the house smell fantastic!

My daughter left home to make her way in the world about 20 years ago. She lived in New York for a long time and then moved to Qatar which is half way around the other side of the world. Needless to say, she didn't get to come home for visits very often. But when she was able to get home for a visit, she always asked me to make this dish for her and her friends. It can be put together a few days in advance and kept in the refrigerator or freezer until you're ready to bake it. Use plastic wrap to cover the dish for storage, not aluminum foil.

As with the other tomato and meat dishes, you'll get the antioxidant benefits of lycopene from the tomatoes and the nerve protection from the vitamin B12 in the meats and eggs.

-- A --
1 lb Italian sausage or bulk pork sausage, crumbled
1 lb ground beef, crumbled
1 - 3 cloves fresh garlic
1 T chopped fresh Italian flat-leaf parsley
1 T chopped fresh basil leaves
small pinch salt (optional)
1 lg can tomatoes (chopped in blender) (about 40 oz.)
Brown meat slowly in deep frying pan. Add remaining "A" ingredients and cook slowly, uncovered, stirring occasionally until most of the liquid has evaporated. About 45 minutes to 1 hour or more depending on how much liquid needs to be evaporated.

-- B --
10 oz lasagna noodles (1 ½ lg pkg)
lg pan of boiling water
Cook noodles in boiling water. Pour into sieve and drain. To keep them from sticking together too much, you can rinse then under the cold water faucet.

-- C --
2 12 oz cartons Riccotta or lg curd cream-style cottage cheese
2 beaten lg eggs
small pinch salt (optional)
some freshly ground black pepper
2 T chopped fresh Italian flat-leaf parsley
½ c grated Parmesan cheese
1 lb Mozzarella (This can either be sliced thin or use the small fresh Mozzarella balls)
Combine all -- C -- ingredients in lg bowl except for the Mozzarella. Mix well.

Place half of the noodles (B) in 13 x 9 x 2" baking dish; spread half the cheese mixture (C) over the noodles; add Mozzarella over all. Spread half the meat mixture (A) over the cheese. Repeat these layers.
Bake in a moderate oven (375°F) for 30 minutes or until the cheese is melted, bubbly, and getting just a bit brown. Remove. Let stand about 10 minutes before cutting.

Enjoy!

Macaroni Salad with Tomatoes, Bell Pepper, and Red Onion

Flavonoids are some of the organic chemicals in plants that act as powerful antioxidants and anticancer agents when eaten by people. Cherry tomatoes are especially rich in flavonoids, which is why I've chosen this particularly delicious macaroni salad for inclusion in this book.

This recipe comes originally from Edward Espe Brown's *Tomato Blessings and Radish Teachings – Recipes and Reflections*, ©1997. It's a beautiful book. I love reading it – even if I don't make all the recipes that he offers.

Here's what you'll need to have on hand:

    1/2 pound macaroni or shell pasta
    1 red onion – thinly sliced
    1 green bell pepper – quartered lengthwise then sliced crosswise
    2 T extra virgin olive oil
    1 pint basket cherry tomatoes, halved
    1/2 T red wine vinegar or balsamic vinegar
    1/2 tsp red chili pepper or Tabasco, to taste
    Pinch Kosher salt or sea salt
    2 T capers (optional)

Cook the macaroni *al dente* in a pot of boiling water. Add the red onion and green pepper and continue cooking for another half-minute. Drain into a colander then transfer to large mixing bowl.

Combine cherry tomatoes with the olive oil, red chili pepper and salt. Add vinegar and capers. Combine with macaroni. Mix, cover, chill. Serves 4 – 6.

Mom's Spaghetti Sauce with Meatballs

I come from a fairly large extended Italian family. My mom always had a big pot of spaghetti sauce bubbling on the back burner of the stove. Many times my brother and sister and I didn't even wait for the spaghetti. We'd put the sauce into a small bowl, dip large chunks of fresh Italian bread into it and eat it just like that. Or, if mom had made meatballs, we could scoop them onto a sliced roll, ladle the sauce over all and have delicious meatball sandwiches.

Tomatoes are rich in lycopene, an antioxidant which has been shown to have anticancer effects for prostate and digestive tract cancers, is linked to a reduced risk of heart attack, and is a useful source of vitamins C and E. For maximum absorption, tomatoes must be heated to release lycopene from the tomato cells. The extra virgin olive oil also helps the body absorb lycopene.

I use whole wheat pasta instead of regular white pasta. It has a lower glycemic index which means it breaks down slower and won't cause a spike in blood sugar. It's also higher in fiber so you have a feeling of being full without eating and eating and eating.

Spaghetti Sauce
    1 lg onion, chopped
    3 T extra virgin olive oil
    2 cloves garlic
    3 1-pound cans tomatoes (6 cups)
    2 8-oz cans seasoned tomato sauce (2 cups)
    1/4 cup chopped fresh flat-leaf Italian parsley leaves (save stems to use in soup)
    1 1/2 T fresh oregano, chopped
    1/4 tsp sea salt

1 tsp fresh thyme
1 - 2 bay leaves
1 - 2 cups spring water
..... Parmesan cheese, grated

Cook onion in hot oil till golden. Add garlic. Brown lightly. Add remaining ingredients. Simmer uncovered 2 1/2 - 3 hours. Remove bay leaves. Serve over hot, cooked spaghetti. Sprinkle with Parmesan cheese.

Meatballs
1 pound ground beef
1/4 pound ground pork
2 slices bread, crumbled in bowl
1/4 cup whole milk
1/2 cup grated Parmesan cheese
1 T Fresh flat-leaf Italian parsley leaves, chopped
1 clove garlic, minced
2 well-beaten eggs
Pinch, salt and pepper
Extra virgin olive oil for browning meatballs in frying pan

Pour milk over bread to moisten. Add remaining ingredients - except olive oil. Mix thoroughly. Form into medium size balls. Brown all sides in hot oil. Add to spaghetti sauce. Let simmer in sauce until ready to serve.

The meat and eggs contain vitamin B12, an essential vitamin which the body is incapable of making on its own. We must get B12 from our food. B12 helps protect nerve fibers.

Tomato Avocado Salad

Tomatoes and avocados go together beautifully and each one compliments the other in terms of color and flavor and texture. This is one of my family's favorite snacks. It's also good as a side dish at breakfast or dinner.

While tomatoes primarily help protect your health with anticancer properties, avocados have antioxidants to help protect from "bad" cholesterol – LDL. The monounsaturated fats in avocados contain vitamins B6 and C and contribute to absorption of vitamins C and E, vitamins that are in tomatoes. Eating both avocado and tomato have a heart-healthy effect on your body.

The extra virgin olive oil along with the avocado provides monounsaturated fats which help your body absorb fat soluble vitamin E. Vitamin E acts as an antioxidant and is also useful in helping to boost the immune system to help you fight off invading bacteria.

Did you know that monounsaturated fat can be directly burned as fuel by your body? All other fats need to be stored before they can be used as fuel.

Here's what you'll need to prepare this easy-to-make, easy-to-eat salad:

   Ripe avocado – not too soft, peeled, pitted, sliced
   Ripe tomato – also not too soft, sliced
   Fresh or dried sweet basil leaves, minced or crumbled
   Fresh or dried oregano leaves, minced
   Fresh or dried flat-leaf Italian parsley leaves, minced
   Extra virgin olive oil

Balsamic vinegar
Garlic powder
Freshly ground black pepper

Arrange the avocado and tomato slices on a plate. Drizzle with extra virgin olive oil and balsamic vinegar. Sprinkle the basil, oregano, parsley, garlic and black pepper over all. Enjoy!

Tomato Bisque

This is an easy and quick-to-make soup as it can be thrown together in 5 minutes and it always tastes good.

As with everything 'tomato', you get vitamins C and E, fiber, anticancer effects, heart protection, and lycopene because the tomatoes are being heated. The lycopene helps protect against prostate cancer.

Here's what you'll need:
  1 lg can tomatoes
  Pinch baking soda to reduce the acidity of the canned tomatoes
  1 small yellow onion, sliced
  Salt and pepper, to taste
  1 cup light cream
  1 - 2 T unsalted butter

Bring the tomatoes to a boil. Add a pinch of baking soda. Add the onion. Add the cream and heat thoroughly. Before serving, remove the onion and add 1 - 2 T butter. Serves 4 - 6.

Tomato Pie

Potatoes are a rich source of good energy and a useful source of vitamin C and iron. Cut off any green or sprouted areas as these are toxic

I'm recommending the red new potatoes as opposed to the other varieties because their glycemic index is lower. This means they don't tend to spike the blood sugar level like some of the others can.

Here's what you need to have on hand to make this dish:

Place in casserole baking dish:
    4 – 5 ripe red tomatoes, sliced
    Flat leaf parsley leaves, minced (save stems for soup)
    1 small yellow onion, chopped
    1 small cucumber, sliced thin
    1 T unsalted butter
    1 tsp sugar
    Salt and pepper to taste

Cover with:
    2 cups mashed potatoes

Sprinkle with:
    3 T grated American cheese

Bake in moderate oven (375°F) until nicely browned.

How to Make Mashed Potatoes
Place in pot of water:
    4 – 5 large red skin new potatoes, peeled and cubed

Bring to boil and cook until potatoes can be easily pierced with fork.
Drain.
Add some milk and unsalted butter.
Mash with potato masher.

And finally ....

Tomato Sandwich

Simple – simple – simple. But very tasty. This is an easy throw-together meal when you don't know what else to eat. It's a staple stand-by for my kids.

Vitamins C and E are prominent in the tomatoes. Vitamin E is a fat soluble vitamin, which means vitamin E needs a fat in order to carry it into the body. In this recipe, butter and mayonnaise fill this roll.

Here's what you'll need:
    Tomato, sliced
    Butter
    Mayonnaise
    Bread, 2 slices

Spread butter and mayonnaise on 1 slice of bread. Add the sliced tomato. Cover with 2nd slice of bread. Pick it up and eat it. Messy, but worth it.

# # #

EXCERPT FROM: *How to Eat Healthy – foods to eat . . . foods to avoid* by Joyce Zborower

When food is plentiful, what constitutes

CONTEMPORARY MALNUTRITION

When a layperson hears the term 'malnutrition', we generally see in our mind's eye the picture of a person, child or adult, with rail-thin limbs, a swollen abdomen, and flies crawling all over his/her face and into the eyeballs. The person has no energy with which to raise their arm to shoo them away. However, this is only one side of malnutrition. The other is obesity. Both are deleterious. Malnutrition, therefore, can be defined as any significant nutritional deviation from that which promotes healthy bodily functioning.

Malnutrition of the body, i.e. the whole organism, begins with malnutrition of the individual cells that make up that body.

The current, traditional model for identifying malnutrition is:

Maltutrition: an insufficiency of one or more nutritional elements necessary for health and well being
-- Primary Malnutrition -- Caused by
-- (1) unavailable foodstuffs (as in poor economy, drought, or over population)
-- (2) when food is plentiful, by poor eating habits

Secondary Malnutrition -- Caused by failure of absorption of essential nutrients
i.e. - the body cannot *use* the nutrients that are available in the foods
-- (1) as in diseases of the gastrointestinal tract, thyroid, kidney, liver, or pancreas
-- (2) by increased nutritional requirements (growth, injuries, burns, surgical procedures, pregnancy, lactation, or fever); or
-- (3) by excessive excretion (diarrhea)

This model needs to be revised to include under 'Primary Malnutrition':
-- (3) when food is plentiful **but essentially devoid of natural micro-nutrients.**

Micro-nutrients are the vitamins, minerals, phyto-chemicals, flavinoids, etc. that are present in fresh, natural, unprocessed foods. They are very delicate and are easily destroyed by heat, refining, and other processing procedures as well as by some agricultural practices.

Macro-nutrients are the fats, carbohydrates and proteins that provide the calories your body either stores as fat or uses for energy. They are very stable and not easily destroyed or altered.

When nutrition gurus talk about "nutrients", they are usually referring to the **macro-** variety – and this is where the confusion arises. Since natural food consists of BOTH micro- and macro-nutrients, and their functions in the body are very different, and you CAN eat one without the other (as in highly refined products), I think it is vitally important that professionals be very specific about which type of nutrient they're talking about.

What is the reasoning behind this proposed change?

From the beginnings of food cultivation, around 10,000 B.C., until 1840 A.D. when Liebeg introduced his NPK (nitrogen, phosphorous, potassium) theory of plant growth, the only foods (from among the hundreds of ingredients available) that were routinely consumed in the refined state (natural nutrient content either severely reduced or eliminated) were: refined sugar (dating from prior to 510 B.C.), refined white wheat flour (dating from prior to 150 B.C.), and refined olive oils, another ancient practice. The production of olive oil began around 5,000 B.C., but I have not yet found a definitive date for when it began to be widely used as a refined product. These were, and are, staple foods.

When these were the primary natural micro-nutrient deficient foods consumed on a regular basis, the impact to the nutrition of the cells was low. (Food preservation, another ancient practice, also somewhat reduced natural micro-nutrient content but not nearly as severely as refining.) The ingestion of a greater majority of untreated, micro-nutrient-rich foods has the effect of "making up for" the nutrient deficiencies of the treated foods.

It is postulated that sugars entering the cells that do not contain sufficient natural micro-nutrients to adequately nourish the cells and provide energy for the work that the cells must do to sustain health and life causes the cells to suffer minute, discreet, cumulative damage that, over time, results in the overt symptoms of what we now call a food related disease.

Food related diseases are: cancer, hyper-tension (high blood pressure), kidney disease, heart disease, obesity (which is not really a disease), diabetes, stroke, and high cholesterol (which I also don't consider to be a disease).

Historically, only the most genetically susceptible individuals exhibited overt symptoms of food related disease, i.e. diabetes and kidney disease – both ancient diseases.

With the advent of chemical agriculture, the micro-nutrient value of all foods produced by this method was slightly reduced. As these foods were fed to animals that were used as food, the micro-nutrient value of those foods for those of us higher on the food chain was also reduced slightly. (Do you see how this is becoming negatively cumulative?)

#

This is the end of this excerpt.

Check out: *How to Eat Healthy – foods to eat . . . foods to avoid* at Amazon.com

Kindle Recipes

3 Fruit Pie Recipes – apple, cherry, crisp persimmon

BBQ Spare Ribs Recipe – succulent fall off the bone with homemade honey BBQ sauce

13 Easy Tomato Recipes – Nature's Lycopene Rich Superfood for Heart Health and Cancer Protection

-- FOOD/NUTRITION RELATED BOOKS

No Work Vegetable Gardening – for in-ground, raised, or container gardening

How To Eat Healthy – foods to eat . . . foods to avoid

The Truth About Olive Oil – benefits, curing methods, remedies

External Uses of Extra Virgin Olive Oil – Folk Remedies ... Body Lotions ... Pet Treatments

Signs of Vitamin B12 Deficiencies – Who's at Risk – Why – What Can Be Done

Disclaimer

The recipes in this book are for informational and educational purposes only. They are not intended to treat or diagnose any medical condition. The author is not a licensed health care professional. Her education and degrees are in the area of clinical psychology though she has had college level training in nutrition.

The author accepts NO responsibility and No liability for your use of any information presented in this book.

One Last Thing

We would love to get your feedback about our book:

If you enjoyed this book or found it useful, we would be very grateful if you would post a short review on Amazon. Your support really does make a difference and we read all of the reviews personally, so we can get your feedback and make our books even better.

If you would like to leave a review, all you need to do is click the review link on this book's page on Amazon.

References

Schmutz, Ervin M. and Lucretia Breazeale Hamilton. *Plants That Poison: an illustrated guide for the American Southwest*. © 1979. Pp. 212-213.

Sunset Western Garden Book. © 2001.

http://blogs.mcm.edu/sncs/?p=241

http://www.answers.com/topic/poisoning-health

http://www.healthchecksystems.com/antioxid.htm

Zborower, Joyce. *How to Eat Healthy – foods to eat . . . foods to avoid* © 2012.

Printed in Great Britain
by Amazon